Tiny Baby
Kangaroos

by Bob Dannon

 HOUGHTON MIFFLIN   BOSTON

PHOTOGRAPHY CREDITS: Cover © Brakefield Photo; 1 © Biosphoto/Ruoso Cyril/Peter : 2 © Jochen Schlenker/Radius Images; 3 © Mitsuaki Iwago/Minden Pictures; 4 © Mitsuaki Iwago/Minden Pictures; 5 © Biosphoto/Ruoso Cyril/Peter; 6 © David Maitland/Getty Images; 7 © Brakefield Photo; 8 © Rosenfeld/Corbis; 9 © Jason Edwards/National Geographic/Getty Images; 10 © Peter Fakler/Alamy

Printed in China

ISBN-13: 978-0-547-02995-5
ISBN-10: 0-547-02995-0

2 3 4 5 6 7 8 9 0940 15 14 13 12 11 10

baby kangaroo

pouch

Kangaroos are animals that
live in Australia.
Every mother kangaroo has a
pouch on the front of her body.
A pouch is like a soft pocket.
A baby kangaroo lives in its
mother's pouch after it is born.

joey

Baby Kangaroos

A young kangaroo is a joey.
A joey crawls into its mother's
pouch after it is born.
A joey cannot see or hear.
A joey is as small as the nail
on your finger.

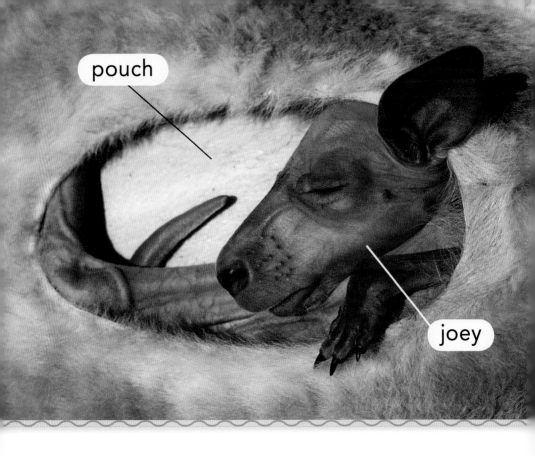

pouch

joey

The First Few Months

A mother kangaroo's pouch
keeps the joey safe and warm.
A joey grows in the pouch.
After a few months, a joey
grows ears, legs, and soft fur.

A Joey Leaves the Pouch

As a joey grows bigger, it begins to move in the pouch. When a joey is six or eight months old, it comes out of the pouch for a few minutes. Then the joey goes back in the pouch.

A Joey Hops

A joey grows and grows.
It follows its mother
through the grass.
The joey learns how to hop.

mother

A joey goes in its mother's pouch when it is scared or tired. Sometimes a mother kangaroo has two joeys. Then the big joey lives in the pouch with the tiny joey. The two joeys share the pouch.

A Joey Grows

A joey drinks milk from its mother's pouch until a joey is one year old.

Then a big joey can find food out of the pouch.

It is now as big as its mother.

kangaroo family

Some girl kangaroos live with their mothers.
When the girl kangaroos have their own joeys, the kangaroo family lives together.

Most boy kangaroos do not
live with their mothers.
They hop away.
They look for other kangaroos
and start a new family.

Responding

How does the mother kangaroo's pouch help the baby kangaroo? Make a chart. List three ways.

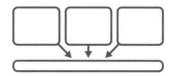

Write About It

Text to World Draw a picture of a baby kangaroo and its mother. Write a sentence about the baby kangaroo.

✔ **TARGET SKILL** **Conclusions**

Use details to figure out more about the text.

✔ **TARGET STRATEGY** **Visualize**

Picture what is happening as you read.

GENRE Informational text gives facts about a topic.